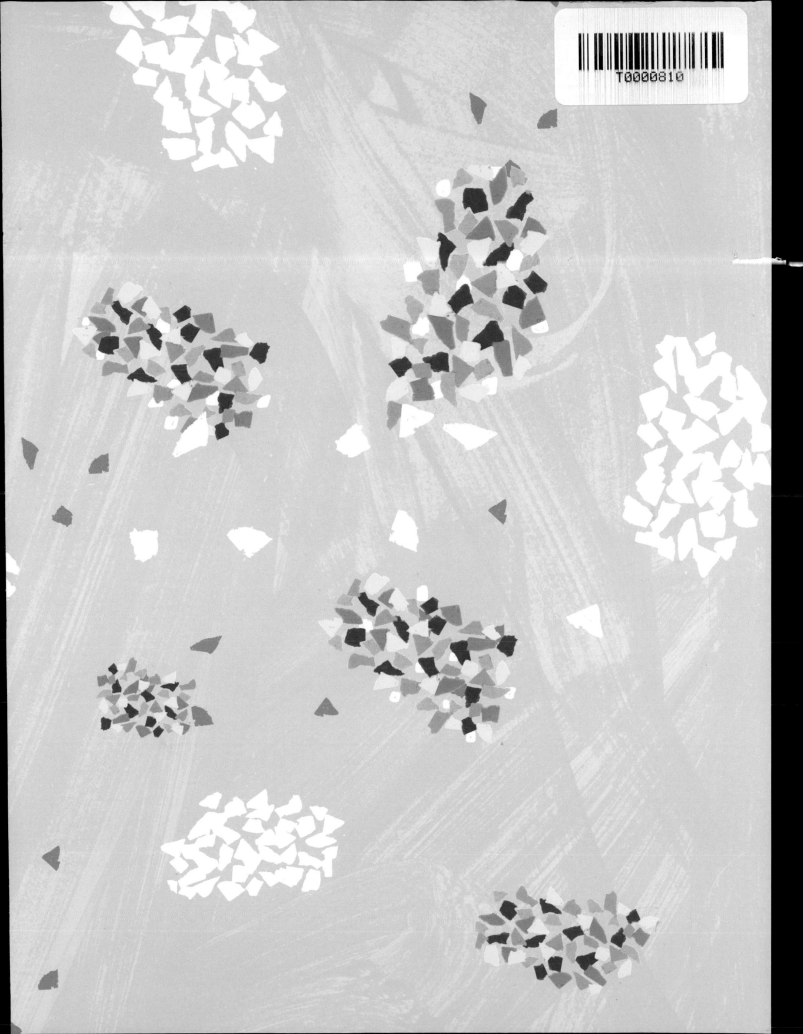

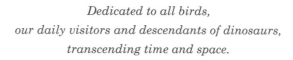

Dedicated to all birds,
our daily visitors and descendants of dinosaurs,
transcending time and space.

Many thanks to Andrew Rubenfeld for his
ornithological expertise.

Published by
Princeton Architectural Press
202 Warren Street
Hudson, New York 12534
www.papress.com

Copyright © 2022 Andrea D'Aquino
All rights reserved.

Printed in China
25 24 23 22 4 3 2 1

ISBN 978-1-64896-050-5

Published by arrangement with Debbie Bibo Agency

This book was illustrated with hand-painted collaged paper, oil pastel, and pencil.

Editors: Rob Shaeffer and Stephanie Holstein
Designer: Andrea D'Aquino

Library of Congress Control Number: 2020950573

SHE HEARD the BIRDS

THE STORY of FLORENCE MERRIAM BAILEY
PIONEERING NATURE ACTIVIST

ANDREA D'AQUINO

PRINCETON ARCHITECTURAL PRESS • NEW YORK

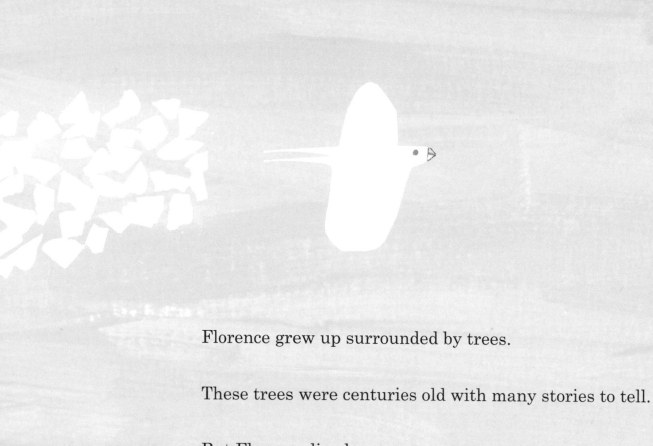

Florence grew up surrounded by trees.

These trees were centuries old with many stories to tell.

But Florence lived many years ago,
so even the trees were a bit younger then.

When she was little, her father took Florence
and her brother on a camping trip that lasted
an entire summer.

The world felt magical, and she enjoyed talking
with forest creatures all day long.

She learned about the stars and planets
from her mother, who was an astronomer.
It was quite unusual for a woman to study
science in those days.

The world

was very

different then.

Florence was especially fascinated by birds, always
wondering where they came from and where they were going.

She dreamed of flying with them high above the treetops.

She patiently learned all of their unique
songs and languages, so she could
understand what the birds were saying.
She had the feeling

        they

           had

                something

                        important

                            to

                              tell

                                her.

One day when she was older, Florence
visited the big city and she saw lots
and lots of rare birds.

But these birds were NOT on trees.

People thought wearing birds
on hats looked beautiful.

To Florence, those hats were
the ugliest things she had ever seen.

In order to help the birds, Florence knew
she had to learn everything about them.

Learning about birds meant being quiet —
listening, waiting, and watching.

She heard the birds.
And they were calling for her to do something.

TOOLS FLORENCE USED FOR BIRD-WATCHING:

A camera to catalog her sightings

A notebook to record her observations

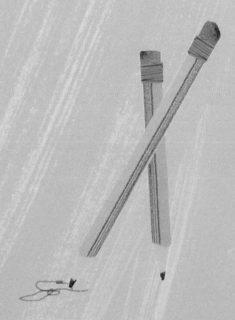

Pencils to write down
or draw her discoveries

Binoculars to see birds up close
without disturbing them

One of her most useful tools was quite simple.

In fact, she had two of them.

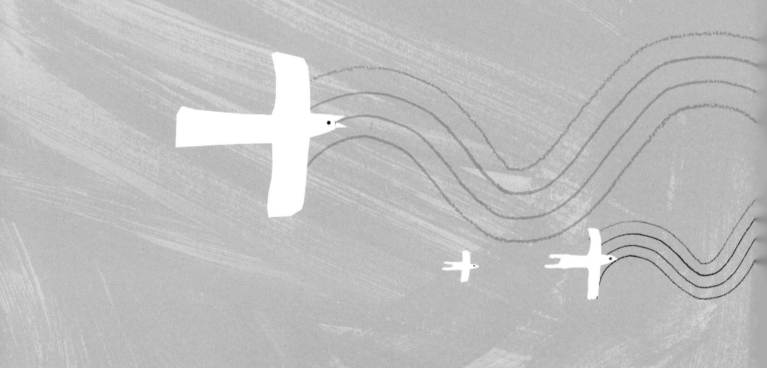

But what was that sound?
Florence learned that some bird-watchers
used guns to shoot birds in order to
study them. This was one of the worst
sounds she had ever heard.

Florence knew that if she was to make a difference, she had to dream big. She felt so sad and hopeless sometimes that she just wanted to fly away.

But the birds told her she had more work to do. Florence decided to share everything she was learning about her feathered friends, so that others could hear what she heard.

"Cheep Cheep"
Sparrow

"Jay! Jay! Jay!"
Blue Jay

"Tweetie tweet tweet"
Goldfinch

"Chick-a-dee, dee, dee"
Black-Capped Chickadee

"Chick chick breee!"
Scarlet Tanager

"Coo-coooo, Coo-cooo!"
Burrowing Owl

"Hee ha wha, hee ha wheee"
Red-Eyed Vireo

"Cheer up, cheer up, cheerio!"
Robin

"Caw! Caw! Caw!"
Crow

"Dearie Dearie"
Wood Pewee

Florence refused to give up. She wrote many books,
including one of the first field guides to American birds, identifying
all kinds of birds and describing how they communicate.

One of her most important suggestions
was to use binoculars to see birds up close.
There would be no need for guns
once people saw things Florence's way.

She taught people how to observe
birds in nature. They saw that the
more common types of birds were
just as fascinating as the rare ones.

Shhhhhhh! Listen.

What are they saying?

cheeep!

oookeel!

Be A FRIEND to BIRDS!

Soon, there were even more beautiful sounds in the air. But this time, they came from people! They were raising their voices, and things began to change.

This time, it was Florence's call that had finally been heard.

The world became safer for the birds, and more beautiful for us all.

FLORENCE MERRIAM BAILEY

Florence Merriam Bailey was born in 1863 in Locust Grove, New York. Growing up, Florence and her siblings were encouraged to explore the wild surrounds of their family's estate. Their early immersion in the outdoors had a lifelong impact on both Florence, who became a pioneering bird activist, and her brother, Clinton, who served as a founder of the National Geographic Society.

Florence's first public efforts to protect birds arose during her student days at Smith College. Not long after the Civil War, a trend took hold among stylish women in the United States and Europe, and hats decorated with exotic plumage of birds became all the rage. The hats were adorned not just with feathers but often with the full carcasses of blue jays, woodpeckers, and even large birds like eagles and turkeys. The production of these hats was a lucrative business, but it came at a high cost: the deaths of an estimated five million birds a year.

In 1889, driven by an extreme distaste for this popular fashion, Bailey and several of her classmates took action. Over the next few years, the group swayed habits, encouraging a boycott of bird-decorated hats that dealt a blow to the sizable industry that manufactured them.

Bailey applied the same social consciousness to the scientific study of birds, known as ornithology, advocating for observing birds in nature rather than in a lab. After her marriage to naturalist Vernon Bailey, the pair went on many camping trips to learn about the flora and fauna of the United States and recorded countless field notes.

Bailey became the first woman fellow of the American Ornithologists' Union in 1929, and she was later awarded its Brewster Medal for her book *Birds of New Mexico* (1928). She authored ten books, including *Birds Through an Opera-Glass* (1889) and the *Handbook of Birds of the Western United States* (1902).

BIRDS STILL NEED OUR HELP

Scientists report that there are nearly three billion fewer birds in North America now than there were fifty years ago. Described as a "full-blown crisis" by the president of the National Audubon Society, this population loss has affected both rare and common species—those we've long enjoyed seeing and hearing in parks and in our own backyards. The draining of wetlands, plowing of fields, spraying of pesticides, and building of skyscrapers, among other factors, have taken a drastic toll on the natural habitats of wild birds.

Perhaps we can learn from Bailey. On your next walk, pause and close your eyes. Can you hear a bird singing? Point to where the song is coming from. Bring along a pair of binoculars to see the birds up close. How many birds can you spot? When we simply take the time to observe our feathered friends, we become more respectful of our environment. Sometimes, just observing can be the start of real change!

RESOURCES

No Woman Tenderfoot: Florence Merriam Bailey, Pioneer Naturalist by Harriet Kofalk
Women in the Field: America's Pioneering Women Naturalists by Marcia Myers Bonta

NORTH AMERICA

Sibley, Peterson, and the National Audubon Society offer comprehensive regional field guides for birders of all levels.

All About Birds from the Cornell Lab of Ornithology
www.allaboutbirds.org

National Audubon Society
www.audubon.org

UNITED KINGDOM

Royal Society for the Protection of Birds
www.rspb.org.uk

British Trust for Ornithology
www.bto.org

AUSTRALIA

Birds SA
birdssa.asn.au

Australian Bird Study Association
absa.asn.au

NEW ZEALAND

Birds New Zealand
www.birdsnz.org.nz

Opposite: Portrait of Florence Merriam Bailey.
Record Unit 7417, Florence Merriam Bailey Papers, 1865–1942.
Courtesy of the Smithsonian Institution Archives.